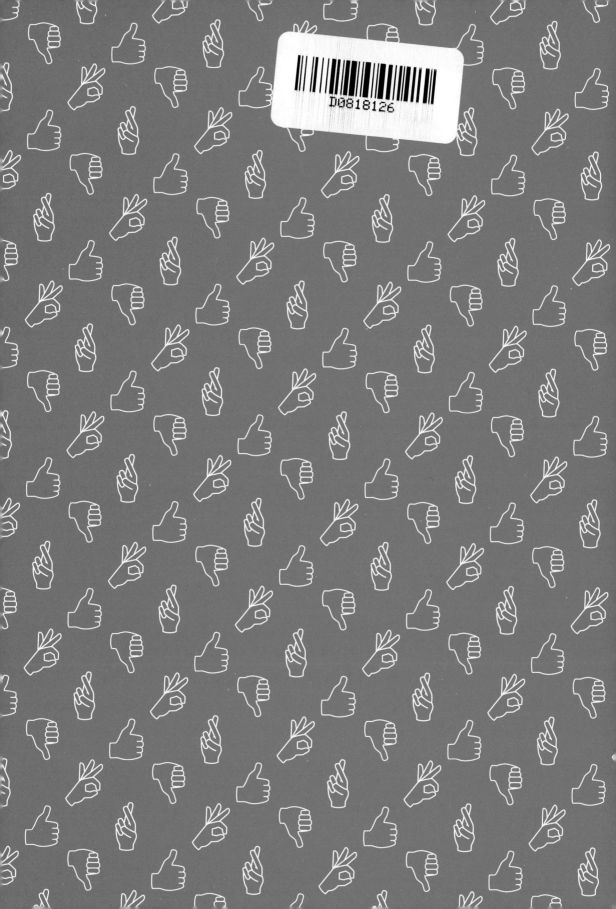

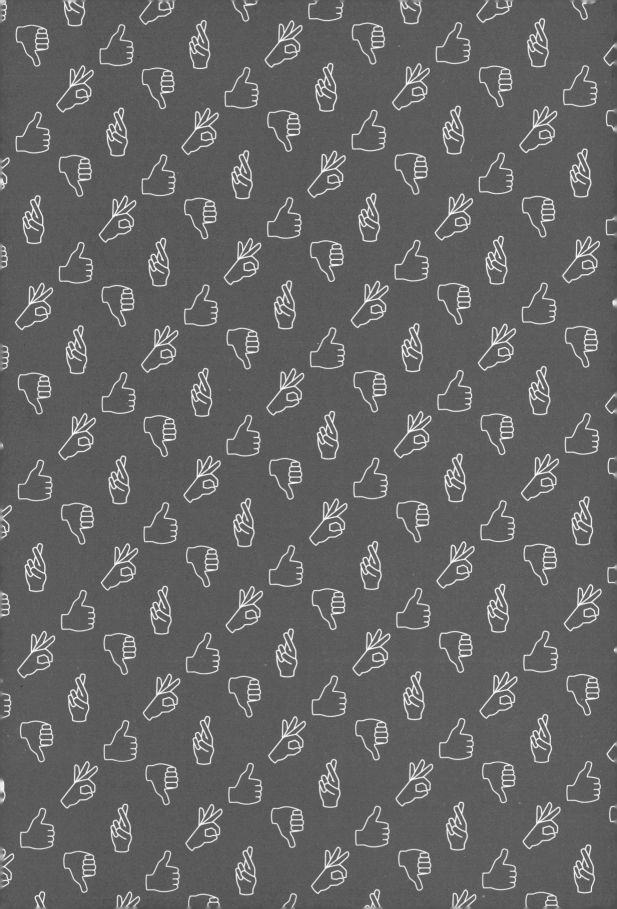

IT'S GONNA BE OKAY

KNOCK KNOCK®
VENICE, CALIFORNIA

Created and published by Knock Knock
1635-B Electric Ave.
Venice, CA 90291
knockknockstuff.com

ISBN: 978-160106409-7
UPC: 825703-50026-4

20 19 18 17

WHAT IF

IT *DOESN'T* ALL WORK OUT?

That's the question that keeps you up at night, causes bitten fingernails, and inspires a nagging anxiety about what happens next. Despite your misgivings, however, some part of you clings tenaciously to the notion that regardless of past (and utterly damning) evidence, it—*you*—will be okay in the end. In the words of the late, great Bob Marley, you're just hoping "every little thing gonna be all right."

Whether it comes naturally or through sheer stubbornness, for better or worse you're stuck with the persistent condition that poets and psychiatrists alike refer to as optimism. When life gives you lemons, you make lemonade—even if you have to spike it with vodka. The clichés mount in defiance of the setbacks you face on both a large scale (economic turmoil, environmental catastrophe, the very existence of mothers-in-law) and a smaller, more personal one (getting overlooked for a promotion, choosing the wrong socks, yet another overdraft fee).

The good news is you're not alone. Most of us are just trying to get through the day, hoping for the best. And it seems we're in very good historical company. Luminaries who self-identified as eternal optimists include Thomas Edison, Helen

Keller, the current Dalai Lama, and even Michael J. Fox. While it's true many of life's ups and downs are out of our control, it's also true that we can choose to enjoy the ride. Experts cited in a study in *Scientific American* contend that the more outgoing, relaxed, and open people are—all traits of the optimist—the more likely they are to encounter new opportunities and to recognize them when they do.

While looking on the bright side may lack the material impact promised in self-help tomes such as *The Secret*, one thing is for sure: according to the *Journal of Happiness Studies,* contentment is a marker for longevity in healthy populations, and is as beneficial for you as smoking is detrimental. At the very least, then, remaining upbeat helps ensure you're around to see it all play out until the (perhaps bitter) end.

Given that you now have a lengthy future ahead of you, how can you maximize your proverbial bowl of cherries? According to an article in *Psychological Science,* it's important to remember that life is still relatively short: those who are reminded that a pleasant experience will end soon are motivated to enjoy it and participate more wholeheartedly. And what better place to revel in the transitory pleasures of existence than in this very journal? Whether you wish to record past triumphs, plan future victories, or simply sketch out the small things that make you smile, you now have a private spot for your treasured Pollyanna poetics that can't be dampened by others' pessimistic counterpoints.

As noted self-help guru Deepak Chopra claims, "Journaling is one of the most powerful tools we have to transform our lives." In addition to helping put one's mind at ease, journal writing has been shown to aid physical health. According to a widely cited study by James W. Pennebaker and Janel D. Seagal, "Writing about important personal experiences in an emotional way... brings about improvements in mental and physical health." Proven benefits include better stress management, strengthened immune systems, fewer doctor visits, and improvement in chronic illnesses such as asthma. (Because sometimes even the most positive attitude doesn't make it any easier to breathe easy.)

It's not entirely clear how journaling accomplishes all this. Catharsis is involved, but many also point to the value of organizing experiences into a cohesive narrative. According to *Newsweek,* some experts believe that journaling "forces us to transform the ruminations cluttering our minds into coherent stories." Writing about life can help you clarify what there is to feel hopeful about. In many ways, journaling enables us to see beyond the bad stuff so that we, in the words of Johnny Nash, "can see clearly now the rain has gone."

As a devotee of this journal, you most likely already have a (fairly) positive outlook and are willing to build upon it in a consistent and accessible manner. You may doubt that it'll really all be hunky-dory, but you're willing to bet it *might* be. You're also smart enough to know that having a positive attitude isn't always painless—it's a process, much like keeping a journal.

Specialists agree that in order to reap the benefits of journaling you have to stick with it, quasi-daily, for as little as five minutes at a time (at least fifteen minutes, however, is best), even on the days you're downright incapable of seeing the silver lining. Finding regular writing times and comfortable locations can help with consistency. If you find yourself unable to muster a single cheerful sentiment, don't stress. Instead, use the quotes inside this journal as a jumping-off point for observations and explorations. Renowned journaler Anaïs Nin suggests asking yourself, "What feels vivid, warm, or near to you at the moment?" Write whatever comes, and don't criticize it; journaling is a means of self-reflection, not a structured composition. In other words, spew. Finally, determine a home for your journal where you can reference it when you're feeling blue—far away from the chocolate drawer or liquor cabinet.

The great poet Robert Frost once remarked, "In three words I can sum up everything I've learned about life—it goes on." Take it from the man who managed to not only get his poetry *published,* but became a legend by doing so: sometimes things really do work out. Before you know it, your sunny disposition will surface naturally, without prompting, all by itself. Now go forth and find something to look forward to!

There are good days
and there are bad days,
and this is one of them.

LAWRENCE WELK

DATE		

WHAT I'M HANGING HOPE ON TODAY:

_____

_____

_____

_____

_____

_____

_____

_____

_____

_____

_____

_____

_____

_____

_____

_____

_____

_____

_____

_____

_____

_____

_____

_____

_____

_____

PREVAILING OUTLOOK FOR TODAY:

I'm not okay, you're not okay, and that's okay.

ELISABETH KÜBLER-ROSS

WHAT I'M HANGING HOPE ON TODAY:

_____

_____

_____

_____

_____

_____

_____

_____

_____

_____

_____

_____

_____

_____

_____

_____

_____

_____

_____

_____

_____

_____

_____

PREVAILING OUTLOOK FOR TODAY:

If we had no winter, the spring would not be so pleasant.

ANNE BRADSTREET

DATE

WHAT I'M HANGING HOPE ON TODAY:

_____

_____

_____

_____

_____

_____

_____

_____

_____

_____

_____

_____

_____

_____

_____

_____

_____

_____

_____

_____

_____

_____

_____

_____

_____

_____

PREVAILING OUTLOOK FOR TODAY:

God knows, there's enough to worry about without worrying about worrying about things.

———————

EDWARD GOREY

DATE

WHAT I'M HANGING HOPE ON TODAY:

_____
_____
_____
_____
_____
_____
_____
_____
_____
_____
_____
_____
_____
_____
_____
_____
_____
_____
_____
_____
_____
_____
_____
_____
_____
_____
_____
_____

PREVAILING OUTLOOK FOR TODAY:

A positive attitude may not solve all your problems, but it will annoy enough people to make it worth the effort.

HERM ALBRIGHT

WHAT I'M HANGING HOPE ON TODAY:

PREVAILING OUTLOOK FOR TODAY:

Trust yourself.
You know more than
you think you do.

BENJAMIN SPOCK

DATE

WHAT I'M HANGING HOPE ON TODAY:

_____
_____
_____
_____
_____
_____
_____
_____
_____
_____
_____
_____
_____
_____
_____
_____
_____
_____
_____
_____
_____
_____
_____
_____
_____
_____

PREVAILING OUTLOOK FOR TODAY:

"Hope" is the thing with feathers—
That perches in the soul—
And sings the tune without the words—
And never stops—at all.

EMILY DICKINSON

WHAT I'M HANGING HOPE ON TODAY:

_____

_____

_____

_____

_____

_____

_____

_____

_____

_____

_____

_____

_____

_____

_____

_____

_____

_____

_____

_____

_____

_____

_____

_____

_____

_____

PREVAILING OUTLOOK FOR TODAY:

Optimist: Day-dreamer more elegantly spelled.

MARK TWAIN

DATE

WHAT I'M HANGING HOPE ON TODAY:

For after all, the best thing one can do
When it is raining, is to let it rain.

HENRY WADSWORTH LONGFELLOW

WHAT I'M HANGING HOPE ON TODAY:

_____

_____

_____

_____

_____

_____

_____

_____

_____

_____

_____

_____

_____

_____

_____

_____

_____

_____

_____

_____

_____

_____

_____

_____

_____

PREVAILING OUTLOOK FOR TODAY:

It's never too late to have a happy childhood.

TOM ROBBINS

DATE

WHAT I'M HANGING HOPE ON TODAY:

_____

_____

_____

_____

_____

_____

_____

_____

_____

_____

_____

_____

_____

_____

_____

_____

_____

_____

_____

_____

_____

_____

_____

PREVAILING OUTLOOK FOR TODAY:

I told the doctor I was overtired, anxiety-ridden, compulsively active, constantly depressed, with recurring fits of paranoia. Turns out I'm normal.

JULES FEIFFER

DATE

WHAT I'M HANGING HOPE ON TODAY:

PREVAILING OUTLOOK FOR TODAY:

Fear tastes like a rusty knife and do not let her into your house.

JOHN CHEEVER

DATE		

WHAT I'M HANGING HOPE ON TODAY:

_____

_____

_____

_____

_____

_____

_____

_____

_____

_____

_____

_____

_____

_____

_____

_____

_____

_____

_____

_____

_____

_____

_____

_____

_____

_____

_____

_____

_____

PREVAILING OUTLOOK FOR TODAY:

I don't know the key to success, but the key to failure is trying to please everybody.

BILL COSBY

DATE

WHAT I'M HANGING HOPE ON TODAY:

He started to sing as he tackled the thing
That couldn't be done, and he did it.

EDGAR A. GUEST

DATE

WHAT I'M HANGING HOPE ON TODAY:

_____

_____

_____

_____

_____

_____

_____

_____

_____

_____

_____

_____

_____

_____

_____

_____

_____

_____

_____

_____

_____

_____

_____

_____

_____

_____

_____

_____

_____

PREVAILING OUTLOOK FOR TODAY:

Oh, my friend, it is not what they take away from you that counts, it's what you do with what you have left.

HUBERT H. HUMPHREY

WHAT I'M HANGING HOPE ON TODAY:

_____
_____
_____
_____
_____
_____
_____
_____
_____
_____
_____
_____
_____
_____
_____
_____
_____
_____
_____
_____
_____
_____
_____
_____
_____

PREVAILING OUTLOOK FOR TODAY:

When all else fails, you always have delusion.

CONAN O'BRIEN

DATE

WHAT I'M HANGING HOPE ON TODAY:

I am an optimist—it does not seem to be much use being anything else.

WINSTON CHURCHILL

WHAT I'M HANGING HOPE ON TODAY:

_____

_____

_____

_____

_____

_____

_____

_____

_____

_____

_____

_____

_____

_____

_____

_____

_____

_____

_____

_____

_____

_____

_____

_____

_____

PREVAILING OUTLOOK FOR TODAY:

Any happiness you get you've got to make yourself.

ALICE WALKER

WHAT I'M HANGING HOPE ON TODAY:

PREVAILING OUTLOOK FOR TODAY:

Life is always a tightrope or a feather bed.
Give me the tightrope.

EDITH WHARTON

WHAT I'M HANGING HOPE ON TODAY:

_____

_____

_____

_____

_____

_____

_____

_____

_____

_____

_____

_____

_____

_____

_____

_____

_____

_____

_____

_____

_____

_____

_____

_____

PREVAILING OUTLOOK FOR TODAY:

Make it work.

TIM GUNN

DATE		

WHAT I'M HANGING HOPE ON TODAY:

_____

_____

_____

_____

_____

_____

_____

_____

_____

_____

_____

_____

_____

_____

_____

_____

_____

_____

_____

_____

_____

_____

_____

_____

PREVAILING OUTLOOK FOR TODAY:

People who keep stiff upper lips find that it's damn hard to smile.

JUDITH GUEST

WHAT I'M HANGING HOPE ON TODAY:

PREVAILING OUTLOOK FOR TODAY:

It's a good thing to have all the props pulled out from under us occasionally. It gives us some sense of what is rock under our feet, and what is sand.

MADELEINE L'ENGLE

DATE

WHAT I'M HANGING HOPE ON TODAY:

You can't have everything.
Where would you put it?

—————————————

STEVEN WRIGHT

DATE

WHAT I'M HANGING HOPE ON TODAY:

_____

_____

_____

_____

_____

_____

_____

_____

_____

_____

_____

_____

_____

_____

_____

_____

_____

_____

_____

_____

_____

_____

_____

_____

_____

PREVAILING OUTLOOK FOR TODAY:

If you can do a half-assed job of anything, you're a one-eyed man in the kingdom of the blind.

KURT VONNEGUT

DATE

WHAT I'M HANGING HOPE ON TODAY:

_____

_____

_____

_____

_____

_____

_____

_____

_____

_____

_____

_____

_____

_____

_____

_____

_____

_____

_____

_____

_____

_____

_____

_____

_____

PREVAILING OUTLOOK FOR TODAY:

Be strong, be brave, be true. Endure.

DAVE EGGERS

WHAT I'M HANGING HOPE ON TODAY:

_____

_____

_____

_____

_____

_____

_____

_____

_____

_____

_____

_____

_____

_____

_____

_____

_____

_____

_____

_____

_____

_____

_____

_____

_____

_____

_____

_____

PREVAILING OUTLOOK FOR TODAY:

My optimism wears heavy boots and is loud.

HENRY ROLLINS

DATE		

WHAT I'M HANGING HOPE ON TODAY:

_____

_____

_____

_____

_____

_____

_____

_____

_____

_____

_____

_____

_____

_____

_____

_____

_____

_____

_____

_____

_____

_____

_____

_____

_____

PREVAILING OUTLOOK FOR TODAY:

Do what you feel in your heart to be right—for you'll be criticized anyway. You'll be damned if you do, and damned if you don't.

***

ELEANOR ROOSEVELT

DATE		

WHAT I'M HANGING HOPE ON TODAY:

_____

_____

_____

_____

_____

_____

_____

_____

_____

_____

_____

_____

_____

_____

_____

_____

_____

_____

_____

_____

_____

_____

_____

_____

PREVAILING OUTLOOK FOR TODAY:

Life isn't fair. It's just fairer than death, that's all.

WILLIAM GOLDMAN

DATE

WHAT I'M HANGING HOPE ON TODAY:

_____

_____

_____

_____

_____

_____

_____

_____

_____

_____

_____

_____

_____

_____

_____

_____

_____

_____

_____

_____

_____

_____

_____

_____

_____

_____

_____

_____

_____

_____

_____

_____

PREVAILING OUTLOOK FOR TODAY:

Hope is definitely not the same thing as optimism. It is not the conviction that something will turn out well, but the certainty that something makes sense, regardless of how it turns out.

———————————

VÁCLAV HAVEL

DATE

WHAT I'M HANGING HOPE ON TODAY:

_____
_____
_____
_____
_____
_____
_____
_____
_____
_____
_____
_____
_____
_____
_____
_____
_____
_____
_____
_____
_____
_____
_____
_____
_____
_____
_____
_____
_____

PREVAILING OUTLOOK FOR TODAY:

I believe in looking
reality straight in the
eye and denying it.

_____

GARRISON KEILLOR

DATE

WHAT I'M HANGING HOPE ON TODAY:

_____
_____
_____
_____
_____
_____
_____
_____
_____
_____
_____
_____
_____
_____
_____
_____
_____
_____
_____
_____
_____
_____
_____
_____
_____
_____
_____
_____

PREVAILING OUTLOOK FOR TODAY:

Sometimes life hits you in the head with a brick. Don't lose faith.

STEVE JOBS

WHAT I'M HANGING HOPE ON TODAY:

_____

_____

_____

_____

_____

_____

_____

_____

_____

_____

_____

_____

_____

_____

_____

_____

_____

_____

_____

_____

_____

_____

_____

PREVAILING OUTLOOK FOR TODAY:

I can't go on, I'll go on.

SAMUEL BECKETT

	DATE	

WHAT I'M HANGING HOPE ON TODAY:

_____

_____

_____

_____

_____

_____

_____

_____

_____

_____

_____

_____

_____

_____

_____

_____

_____

_____

_____

_____

_____

_____

_____

_____

_____

_____

_____

_____

_____

PREVAILING OUTLOOK FOR TODAY:

I always think that cynics are really romantics who have been crushed sometime in their lives and have put up this cynical mask to protect themselves.

JEFF BRIDGES

DATE

WHAT I'M HANGING HOPE ON TODAY:

_____
_____
_____
_____
_____
_____
_____
_____
_____
_____
_____
_____
_____
_____
_____
_____
_____
_____
_____
_____
_____
_____
_____
_____
_____
_____
_____

PREVAILING OUTLOOK FOR TODAY:

80 percent of life is showing up.

WOODY ALLEN

DATE		

WHAT I'M HANGING HOPE ON TODAY:

_____
_____
_____
_____
_____
_____
_____
_____
_____
_____
_____
_____
_____
_____
_____
_____
_____
_____
_____
_____
_____
_____
_____
_____
_____

PREVAILING OUTLOOK FOR TODAY:

You tried your best, and you failed miserably. The lesson is, 'never try.'

MATT GROENING

WHAT I'M HANGING HOPE ON TODAY:

_____

_____

_____

_____

_____

_____

_____

_____

_____

_____

_____

_____

_____

_____

_____

_____

_____

_____

_____

_____

_____

_____

_____

_____

_____

_____

_____

_____

_____

PREVAILING OUTLOOK FOR TODAY:

We are all in the gutter, but some of us
are looking at the stars.

OSCAR WILDE

WHAT I'M HANGING HOPE ON TODAY:

PREVAILING OUTLOOK FOR TODAY:

Now and then it's good to pause in our pursuit of happiness and just be happy.

GUILLAUME APOLLINAIRE

WHAT I'M HANGING HOPE ON TODAY:

_____

_____

_____

_____

_____

_____

_____

_____

_____

_____

_____

_____

_____

_____

_____

_____

_____

_____

_____

_____

_____

_____

_____

_____

_____

_____

_____

PREVAILING OUTLOOK FOR TODAY:

Rose-colored glasses are never made in bifocals. Nobody wants to read the small print in dreams.

ANN LANDERS

WHAT I'M HANGING HOPE ON TODAY:

_____

_____

_____

_____

_____

_____

_____

_____

_____

_____

_____

_____

_____

_____

_____

_____

_____

_____

_____

_____

_____

_____

_____

_____

_____

_____

_____

_____

_____

_____

PREVAILING OUTLOOK FOR TODAY:

Life is a tragedy when seen in close-up, but a comedy in long-shot.

CHARLIE CHAPLIN

DATE

WHAT I'M HANGING HOPE ON TODAY:

_____
_____
_____
_____
_____
_____
_____
_____
_____
_____
_____
_____
_____
_____
_____
_____
_____
_____
_____
_____
_____
_____
_____
_____

PREVAILING OUTLOOK FOR TODAY:

The problem with self-improvement is knowing when to quit.

DAVID LEE ROTH

DATE

WHAT I'M HANGING HOPE ON TODAY:

_____

_____

_____

_____

_____

_____

_____

_____

_____

_____

_____

_____

_____

_____

_____

_____

_____

_____

_____

_____

_____

_____

_____

_____

_____

_____

PREVAILING OUTLOOK FOR TODAY:

Life is just one damn thing after another.

ELBERT HUBBARD

DATE	

WHAT I'M HANGING HOPE ON TODAY:

PREVAILING OUTLOOK FOR TODAY:

If you are not happy you had better stop worrying about it and see what treasures you can pluck from your own brand of unhappiness.

ROBERTSON DAVIES

DATE

WHAT I'M HANGING HOPE ON TODAY:

We are all special cases.

ALBERT CAMUS

WHAT I'M HANGING HOPE ON TODAY:

_____

_____

_____

_____

_____

_____

_____

_____

_____

_____

_____

_____

_____

_____

_____

_____

_____

_____

_____

_____

_____

_____

_____

_____

_____

_____

_____

_____

_____

PREVAILING OUTLOOK FOR TODAY:

Courage is being scared to death—and saddling up anyway.

JOHN WAYNE

WHAT I'M HANGING HOPE ON TODAY:

_____

_____

_____

_____

_____

_____

_____

_____

_____

_____

_____

_____

_____

_____

_____

_____

_____

_____

_____

_____

_____

_____

_____

_____

_____

_____

_____

_____

PREVAILING OUTLOOK FOR TODAY:

I have an everyday religion that works for me. Love yourself first, and everything else falls into line. You really have to love yourself to get anything done in this world.

LUCILLE BALL

DATE

WHAT I'M HANGING HOPE ON TODAY:

PREVAILING OUTLOOK FOR TODAY:

Isn't it cool when the days that are supposed to feel good, actually do?

—————

JIM CARREY

WHAT I'M HANGING HOPE ON TODAY:

PREVAILING OUTLOOK FOR TODAY:

It's okay is a cosmic truth.

RICHARD BACH

DATE

WHAT I'M HANGING HOPE ON TODAY:

_____

_____

_____

_____

_____

_____

_____

_____

_____

_____

_____

_____

_____

_____

_____

_____

_____

_____

_____

_____

_____

_____

_____

_____

_____

_____

PREVAILING OUTLOOK FOR TODAY:

You've got to take the bitter with the sour.

SAMUEL GOLDWYN

WHAT I'M HANGING HOPE ON TODAY:

PREVAILING OUTLOOK FOR TODAY:

I have hope because what's the alternative to hope? Despair? If you have despair, you might as well put your head in the oven.

STUDS TERKEL

DATE

WHAT I'M HANGING HOPE ON TODAY:

There must be more
to life than having
everything!

MAURICE SENDAK

DATE

WHAT I'M HANGING HOPE ON TODAY:

_____
_____
_____
_____
_____
_____
_____
_____
_____
_____
_____
_____
_____
_____
_____
_____
_____
_____
_____
_____
_____
_____
_____
_____
_____
_____
_____
_____
_____
_____

PREVAILING OUTLOOK FOR TODAY:

The only courage that matters is the kind that gets you from one moment to the next.

MIGNON MCLAUGHLIN

WHAT I'M HANGING HOPE ON TODAY:

_____

_____

_____

_____

_____

_____

_____

_____

_____

_____

_____

_____

_____

_____

_____

_____

_____

_____

_____

_____

_____

_____

_____

_____

_____

_____

PREVAILING OUTLOOK FOR TODAY:

You can't be that kid standing at the top
of the waterslide, overthinking it. You have
to go down the chute.

TINA FEY

DATE

WHAT I'M HANGING HOPE ON TODAY:

_____

_____

_____

_____

_____

_____

_____

_____

_____

_____

_____

_____

_____

_____

_____

_____

_____

_____

_____

_____

_____

_____

_____

_____

_____

_____

_____

PREVAILING OUTLOOK FOR TODAY:

It's hard to beat a person who never gives up.

BABE RUTH

	DATE	

WHAT I'M HANGING HOPE ON TODAY:

_____

_____

_____

_____

_____

_____

_____

_____

_____

_____

_____

_____

_____

_____

_____

_____

_____

_____

_____

_____

_____

_____

_____

_____

_____

PREVAILING OUTLOOK FOR TODAY:

If I had my life to live over...I would have more actual troubles and fewer imaginary troubles.

DON HEROLD

WHAT I'M HANGING HOPE ON TODAY:

PREVAILING OUTLOOK FOR TODAY:

Sometimes I lie awake at night, and I ask, "Where have I gone wrong?" Then a voice says to me, "This is going to take more than one night."

CHARLES M. SCHULZ

DATE

WHAT I'M HANGING HOPE ON TODAY:

One of the keys to happiness is a bad memory.

———

RITA MAE BROWN

WHAT I'M HANGING HOPE ON TODAY:

PREVAILING OUTLOOK FOR TODAY:

It takes ten times as long to put yourself back together as it does to fall apart.

SUZANNE COLLINS

DATE

WHAT I'M HANGING HOPE ON TODAY:

PREVAILING OUTLOOK FOR TODAY:

The purpose of life is to be defeated by greater and greater things.

RAINER MARIA RILKE

DATE	

WHAT I'M HANGING HOPE ON TODAY:

_____

_____

_____

_____

_____

_____

_____

_____

_____

_____

_____

_____

_____

_____

_____

_____

_____

_____

_____

_____

_____

_____

PREVAILING OUTLOOK FOR TODAY:

I understand the concept of optimism.
But I think with me what you
get is a *lack* of cynicism.

———

TOM HANKS

WHAT I'M HANGING HOPE ON TODAY:

PREVAILING OUTLOOK FOR TODAY:

Damn it, how will I ever get out of this labyrinth?

SIMÓN BOLÍVAR

WHAT I'M HANGING HOPE ON TODAY:

PREVAILING OUTLOOK FOR TODAY:

What sane person could live in this world and not be crazy?

URSULA K. LE GUIN

DATE

WHAT I'M HANGING HOPE ON TODAY:

_____

_____

_____

_____

_____

_____

_____

_____

_____

_____

_____

_____

_____

_____

_____

_____

_____

_____

_____

_____

_____

_____

_____

_____

_____

_____

_____

PREVAILING OUTLOOK FOR TODAY:

I like living. I have sometimes been wildly despairing, acutely miserable, racked with sorrow, but through it all I still know quite certainly that just to *be* alive is a grand thing.

AGATHA CHRISTIE

DATE		

WHAT I'M HANGING HOPE ON TODAY:

_____

_____

_____

_____

_____

_____

_____

_____

_____

_____

_____

_____

_____

_____

_____

_____

_____

_____

_____

_____

_____

_____

_____

_____

_____

_____

PREVAILING OUTLOOK FOR TODAY:

You cannot protect yourself from sadness without protecting yourself from happiness.

JONATHAN SAFRAN FOER

	DATE	

WHAT I'M HANGING HOPE ON TODAY:

Start every day off with a smile— and get it over with.

W. C. FIELDS

DATE

WHAT I'M HANGING HOPE ON TODAY:

You may not realize it when it happens,
but a kick in the teeth may be the best thing
in the world for you.

WALT DISNEY

	DATE	

WHAT I'M HANGING HOPE ON TODAY:

_____

_____

_____

_____

_____

_____

_____

_____

_____

_____

_____

_____

_____

_____

_____

_____

_____

_____

_____

_____

_____

_____

_____

PREVAILING OUTLOOK FOR TODAY:

Men can only be happy when they do not assume that the object of life is happiness.

GEORGE ORWELL

WHAT I'M HANGING HOPE ON TODAY:

_____

_____

_____

_____

_____

_____

_____

_____

_____

_____

_____

_____

_____

_____

_____

_____

_____

_____

_____

_____

_____

_____

_____

_____

_____

_____

_____

PREVAILING OUTLOOK FOR TODAY:

I have a plan— to go mad.

FYODOR DOSTOEVSKY

WHAT I'M HANGING HOPE ON TODAY:

_____

_____

_____

_____

_____

_____

_____

_____

_____

_____

_____

_____

_____

_____

_____

_____

_____

_____

_____

_____

_____

_____

_____

_____

_____

PREVAILING OUTLOOK FOR TODAY:

Go on failing. Go on.
Only next time, try to
fail better.

SAMUEL BECKETT

DATE

WHAT I'M HANGING HOPE ON TODAY:

PREVAILING OUTLOOK FOR TODAY:

Follow your passion. Stay true to yourself.
Never follow someone else's path unless
you're in the woods and you're lost and see a
path. By all means, you should follow that.

ELLEN DEGENERES

DATE

WHAT I'M HANGING HOPE ON TODAY:

PREVAILING OUTLOOK FOR TODAY:

So, this is my life. And I want you to know that I am both happy and sad and I'm still trying to figure out how that could be.

_____

STEPHEN CHBOSKY

DATE

WHAT I'M HANGING HOPE ON TODAY:

Let other pens dwell on guilt and misery.

JANE AUSTEN

DATE		

WHAT I'M HANGING HOPE ON TODAY:

_____

_____

_____

_____

_____

_____

_____

_____

_____

_____

_____

_____

_____

_____

_____

_____

_____

_____

_____

_____

_____

_____

_____

_____

_____

_____

PREVAILING OUTLOOK FOR TODAY:

The truth will set you free. But not until it is finished with you.

DAVID FOSTER WALLACE

DATE		

WHAT I'M HANGING HOPE ON TODAY:

PREVAILING OUTLOOK FOR TODAY:

I'm a kind of paranoiac in reverse. I suspect people of plotting to make me happy.

J. D. SALINGER

DATE		

WHAT I'M HANGING HOPE ON TODAY:

_____

_____

_____

_____

_____

_____

_____

_____

_____

_____

_____

_____

_____

_____

_____

_____

_____

_____

_____

_____

_____

_____

_____

PREVAILING OUTLOOK FOR TODAY:

Everything has been figured out, except how to live.

JEAN-PAUL SARTRE

WHAT I'M HANGING HOPE ON TODAY:

_____

_____

_____

_____

_____

_____

_____

_____

_____

_____

_____

_____

_____

_____

_____

_____

_____

_____

_____

_____

_____

_____

_____

_____

PREVAILING OUTLOOK FOR TODAY:

It's like singing on a boat during a terrible storm at sea. You can't stop the raging storm, but singing can change the hearts and spirits of the people who are together on that ship.

ANNE LAMOTT

DATE

WHAT I'M HANGING HOPE ON TODAY:

Life is either a daring adventure or nothing.

HELEN KELLER

WHAT I'M HANGING HOPE ON TODAY:

PREVAILING OUTLOOK FOR TODAY:

Everything is going to work out just fine.
Probably.

———————

KNOCK KNOCK